dusk before dawn

carys maloney

to my beautiful
friend yasmine,
one of the strongest
people i know.

don't write me off
if you haven't bothered
to read my story.

- p r e j u d i c e

i am changing
growing constantly,
a work in progress
i am not the same
day by day
or in every situation
sometimes, i am my antithesis
sensitive and invincible
kind yet powerful
this doesn't mean i am fake
rather, it makes me real
i don't think i can define myself
and maybe, that's okay.

- p a r a d o x

you put yourself through the pain
this world has caused you
to cope with it all.

- it won't always be like this

strength
in its rawest form
is standing back up
your feet placed
not firmly, but
shaking rather
on rock bottom
taking a deep breath,
hands trembling
as you delicately begin
to rebuild yourself.

- i am so proud of you

to have a closed mind
is to shut yourself off
from an infinite amount of
possibilities.
to have an open mind
is to accept you don't know all
and in return
revel in the knowledge
of all that could be.

- s t a y o p e n

i sleep in a rose bed
thoughts winding round my head
i can make them bloom pretty
or leave them for dead.

- don't feed negativity

everybody tells you
not to lie to others
but nobody seems to mention
the damage that can be caused
by lying to yourself.

-   d e n i a l

she had a peacefully wild heart craving
nothing but love and adventure; in a life
that lacked this, how can you wonder
why she went mad?

i'm a soft fire
that you should not tame
i burn in elegance
i roar in flames
don't fear my warmth
but fear my sting
and the absence of me
caressing your skin
didn't they warn you
to keep your distance?
playing in an inferno with
such persistence
i'll only burn in your memory
engulfing your mind
you may try to erase me
well i'm just not that kind.

- s o f t f i r e

some people are on your level
others aren't
your actions will be
totally plausible to some
yet will seem alien
to others
not everyone will understand
who you are
and the message you bring
but those who do
will marvel,
in your magnificence.

- don't doubt yourself

i thought paradise would be
sunflower filled fields
where every day was blessed
with the glow of white sunshine
or perhaps
golden sands
that spread on for miles
with the distant whisper of an ocean
beckoning me in.
i thought paradise would be
where i was wealthy,
looking grown up and
beautiful
buying whatever took my fancy
without money being an issue.
what i never thought paradise would be
is a feeling.
a feeling of having made it
not in the 'real world'
but to happiness;
still in the same house
the same room
the same bed
where all i used to be able to do
was cry,
and dream of brighter days.

now i realise
paradise
isn't a physical place
but somewhere within myself
where i finally seem to have arrived
and it is better than i ever
could have imagined.

- p a r a d i s e (i t ' s h e r e n o w)

no
love doesn't hurt
rather
its absence does
if love is a drug
and loss,
a possible side effect
then so it is.

-   l o v e w i t h o u t f e a r

when i feel sadness
it's never just an ounce
of emotion
in a passing moment;
it's a hurricane that
hurls me
unexpectedly out of place
sweeping me up, involuntarily
into the heart of an
unforgiving storm
until i seem to become one with it,
entirely
collecting the traumas of everyone
surrounding me
and absorbing them into
my orbit
like how the strong wind carries
the swirling wreckage

needless to say
how i feel,
when i love.

- i m m e r s e d

and i sit here now and wonder
how somebody else could
ever have become
such a huge part of myself.

- i am you no more

like a shadow cast,
from the light of the sun
you can feel put out
overlooked
concealed by the radiant glow
of others around you
don't be intimidated;
instead, lift yourself up
by lifting those around you
walk with the confidence you
wish you had been gifted
and you'll see, you'll realise
one day
passing a mirror by
you are the sun herself
for you bring life
to all those who
encounter you.

-   c h i l d o f t h e s u n

sometimes
the version of someone you once
loved
only exists now
inside your memory
you'll never forget
and though hard to accept
once done so
you'll move on
to live again.

- l e t g o

occasionally, you must put yourself
through temporary discomfort, because you believe
in yourself enough to aim for long-term success.

yes, i am young
but i am also responsible
so please do not belittle me
to make yourself more comfortable.

-    r e s p e c t

if she shares her soul
with you
know that you are blessed
empower her
reciprocate her affection
for you are one of the lucky ones
her love,
is pure and timeless
the kind that people write
songs about
she is a butterfly
you've chased for so long
but you mustn't weigh her down
not now
for she has found her wings
and is no longer afraid
to fly.

-   g o d d e s s

whisper
write
scream
cry
get it out of yourself
and its hold over you
shall weaken.

- e x p r e s s i o n

some people
intentionally or not
will begin to drain you
they'll try to drag you down
into their storm

know that you are separate
you can be there for them
without taking it all on yourself
watch
and be the stillness
amongst the unrest of the people
who are fighting so very hard
knowing it's not just okay
but essential
to preserve yourself and your solitude
for you, too
have fought too hard
for it.

- b a l a n c e is k e y

feelings
are like the voice of the soul
and
just like everyone's voice
they ought to be
acknowledged
respected
and most of all
accepted.

- so, listen

anyone can touch your body
but only few people
can touch your soul
chaos arises when you confuse the two;
one is only temporary
the other,
very much permanent
in a way that never really leaves you
the same as before.

- know the difference

my soul still craves
a person that does not exist anymore
or maybe that time
when life was
a little easier
a little happier
and you just happened
to be by my side
but i guess paths just cross
and don't run parallel
alongside forever
so i let you go
your separate way
and although it hurt
for a long time
i now see this is always how
it was meant to be
for my path
filled with growth and love
lies ahead now
and i shall wander it, discovering myself
along the way.

- when friends break your heart

don't walk all over me
and then expect me
to spring right back up
into your arms
i am worth more
than that.

how tedious and unnatural it is
to feel trapped within your own life
for your daily routine
to have become a vicious cycle,
holding you captive
as its prey
you don't feel happy nor
satisfied
but you tell yourself
you should
doing nothing but make you feel worse
in return
you feel you need a justified reason
to find the courage to make a change
let me tell you that
your discontent
along with the stagnancy around you
is the most valid reason of all
know that life,
just like time
was never meant to stand still
so move on,
walk
crawl
jump in head first
whatever you need to do
just be aware
at any moment you wish,
you can,
take your life back into
your own hands.

- you always had the power

don't follow in someone else's footsteps;
chances are, they will not fit.

i don't understand why
you expect me to attach labels
to myself
i am a human being
with hidden depths of an ocean
surging
just below my skin
and emotions
so vast, so varying
that they mimic the slopes
of the highest mountains.
i cannot be summed up with words
that do not even scratch
my surface.

once you become in tune with
yourself
the world around you seems
to change accordingly
it's as if you've been granted
fresh eyes
as you endlessly notice the little things
that entwine themselves among each day
bringing you moments of joy.
suddenly the signs are everywhere
reminding you that you were
never alone
and you wonder now
with a heart full of gratitude
how you could ever have been
so blind.

-   a p p r e c i a t i o n

i've found ignorance occurs because people tend
to automatically dislike what they don't understand,
instead of seeking to expand their knowledge and
understanding of the world around them.

you were an angel-like figure
always so soft,
with such warmth
almost too pure for
this earth,
at all
so it was no surprise
when you left
how your skin glowed
as you slept
young again once
more
you're a true angel now,
i'm sure.

- n a n n y

the real goal is to
find somebody
your soul vibes so hard with
you rarely need to explain
your actions
for they already know exactly why
you do what you do.

-   h a r m o n y

courage comes in many forms
from risking your life,
your heart
to moving on from a burden
or letting go of doubts
the world may not always celebrate
your courageousness
it may not even seem to notice
these little victories you achieve
each and every day
but i do,
and so should you
a step taken
no matter how 'big' or 'small'
is a huge achievement
that deserves your recognition
more than anyone else's
so applaud yourself
smile, for you know
you are strong, resilient
and able
to grow.

- your bravery is admirable

you long to go back
oh, how it breaks you
to leave it behind again
is the pleasure worth the pain,
in the end?
in my experience, usually yes
good things come to an end
only so we can appreciate them
when they arise again
and they will, they will.

-   s m i l e b e c a u s e i t w a s

a black hole
absorbing all things bleak
morphing you out of shape
inside
it invades every private moment
and eventually
every public one too
distorting your reality
so that all you once loved
now holds little purpose to you
a cruel fate
which too many of us must endure
constantly making us wonder
what it could all be for
but it is grinding you down
so you can build yourself
back up
you are stronger
than you will ever know
and your suffering will soon
leave only love
left to show.

-   y o u a r e s t r o n g e r

hope is essential
it has a tendency to regenerate itself,
when lost
for it is on your side after all
but when associated with pain,
so much pain
it can seem to be absent completely
or numbed deliberately
through fear of wanting better, and
being pushed back down
time
and time
again
even so
please hold tight to it
keep it with you
to keep yourself alive
and you will know
brighter days.

the beauty of art
is that it should not be explained
we can quietly share an appreciation for
its existence;
through perceiving it in different ways,
we can learn things
about ourselves.
art holds its value in mystery
which brings comfort to so many
neither right nor wrong
it simply exists,
admirably
speaking volumes
from a single soul's experience
to the world and beyond.

- we all need art

oh darling
haven't you ever noticed?
all truly lovely things
must face hardships
before they can become
what they really are
roses must suffer the pain of harsh winters
before they can begin to bloom
artists must suffer loss and heartbreak
before they can express these emotions
as masterpieces
and you
you are no different
trust that life
will make you oh so joyous
but first
she must make you humble and
strong.

    -   the sun sets to rise again

maybe they don't smile
because they haven't the energy
to be fake anymore
not because they are rude.
maybe they don't talk
because they have been shut down
too many times in the past
not because they are self-righteous.
maybe they don't volunteer
because they are so scared of being
humiliated again
not because they don't care enough
to even try.
maybe you should take time
to look deeper
before assuming why people
behave as they do today.

you say you act out of love
but i think you act out of fear
you were always so fretful of
the unknown
switching from pity to anger
in an instant
i never know if what you feel
is real
no wonder i was so confused
torn between your world
and his
at least now i have my own thoughts
which i kindly ask for you
not to twist
should i share them with you,
you always seem to make me regret
it is a shame
a sad truth
that through time
i've come to accept.

-   o n l y   s o   d e e p

like vines
about a steel gate
you gradually take your hold over people
so slowly,
you start to grow on them
until
without them even realising
you trap them
under your twisted spell
feeding yourself through their gaps
you make them feel
as if you're that missing piece
they've been searching for
the one that they adore
so they needn't search
anymore

but you seem to forget
as you go about deceiving
vines can be cut back,
cut off
left to rot.
people don't stay unconscious forever
they'll recover their power,
standing so strongly in it
that you'll wither away
their light
shrivelling you up
to become nothing but
a weed
amidst their garden
of eden.

- cut off toxic people

our time here is limited
so don't allow your options to be.

- expand your horizons

how great is it
to travel, to explore
to discover and learn
maybe life wasn't meant to be lived in
one place
not with such an expansive planet
surrounding us
we long to wander it
to uncover places and
find ourselves
and so, we shall.

- w a n d e r l u s t

to do all things through love with
only the purest of intentions is the secret to an
abundance of happiness.

the reason for life
it's been above us
all along
the sky stretching out like a
sparse white canvas
urging us to make what we will of it
in this time we have.

- w e a r e o n l y a m o m e n t

i used to view my sensitivity as
a weakness
but now i know it
only as a strength
for to feel
is to be alive.

- e m p a t h

maturity has little to do with age and a
lot to do with character.

as children
we believe adults know all the answers
about everything
and anything
but as we grow up, we realise
when it comes to the things life
is truly about
adults seem to have forgotten
and it is children who often hold
the most sensible responses.

- m y t h o f g r o w i n g u p a n d k n o w i n g a l l

six months later
and i'm walking the same path again
the stars seemed familiar
just like they were back then
only now i can look up
and the moon seemed to speak
i'm not hiding anymore.
my strength is now radiating
when once,
i had felt so weak
i'm not alone anymore;
it's clear i never was
i just had to feel that way
to know and build myself up
this path leads me home now you see
and it's funny since i'm walking it in
reverse
my life has turned around
so i cry,
because i've made it, here and
now
still under the same sky
but in a whole different world.

- this is real

happiness
it may be closer to your grasp
than you first suspect
stop chasing it
stop running from it
slow down and
listen;
tune into yourself
quietly, gently
and you may even realise
it already resides
within you
right now
for true happiness
is not external, at all.

- it's all within you

once you discover
how to say yes
the world seems to open up
in your favour
it's out there for the taking
but it is yours if you claim it
not if you want it.

- d o n ' t j u s t s u r v i v e

what if
your mind acts as a store
of other people's negative opinions
doubts
and concerns
they have projected onto you
over the years
and your heart
is the essence of who you are
and what you know
to be the truth
through how you feel?
for this reason
following your heart is never foolish
but rather brave
and how to live authentically
in such a world as this
scary as it might be
to do so
it is your truth you are living
it is your lessons you are learning
and your rewards you are reaping
therefore,
you can never really regret
anything.

-   i n t u i t i o n

other people have no place
no right
to plant doubt in your mind
even if it does come from
a place of love
so know there is nothing wrong
with turning your thoughts
the other way;
you don't always have to let the seed
see the light of day.

-   s e e d   o f   d o u b t

all is revealed
under the light of the moon
the truth shall surface,
the pain shall transmute.

- full moon

like a sky encompassed in
greyish clouds
with a crack of blue
visible on the horizon
there is always good amongst
the bad
though it has mastered the art
of disguise
tending to only become visible to us
in retrospect.

- y i n   y a n g

to never take a risk
may help you to survive
but in return, you shall never know
what it is to live.

- risks are inevitable

living in the past
does nothing
but make it the pain of your present
good or bad
it's not real, anymore
let go.

- the past is gone

you took my heart
setting it on fire with
the promise of passion
and danger
yet you watered it down
with doubt and
nothingness
instantly
you cut me back
my tears putting out the fire you
birthed in me
their salt healing my wounds
until your name stung me
no more.

- you can't destroy me

to hate you would imply
i still give my energy to you
don't flatter yourself;
i am free of you in all forms.
i can only hope now
you find a motive to fight the
hatred you must feel
so prominently, in your heart
to have so willingly deceived me
with all your sickening lies
forcing us
to grow apart.

    -   h o p e y o u h e a l , t o o

you frown,
look down at me
like you see me
as beneath you
but how small that makes you
for you cannot see
that the bigger person
stands in front of you.

-    s t a n d d o w n

to be seen but never noticed
to speak but to never be heard
to give but to never receive
it's not hard to become invisible
in a world like this
where extroversion is favoured and
expectations are high
deadlines are set and
empathy is few and far between
fading into the blur of life's fast pace
we learn the tough way that time
does not wait for anyone.
so let time race ahead
along with those
who race to their graves
open your eyes and
be still
for when life is lived,
time is killed.

- ghost girl

happiness takes courage
which i never used to have
in a society that gives us
every reason to be sad
to take the world on
carrying it on our shoulders
it's no wonder we're crazy
growing up before we get older
why the rush?
we are taught to want more
ambition is key
but such a fatal flaw.

- m o m e n t t o m o m e n t

if you respect someone
be honest
it may be the harder option for you
but the truth can save a person
a lot of pain
in the long run.

- the truth is freeing

but without those cloudy nights
we would never appreciate the beauty
of those clear, star-filled skies.

- perspective

people hurt feelings
with words
and music heals souls
with lyrics.

- the power of song

have you ever noticed that
the prettiest star
shines noticeably bright
on and on
despite the darkness surrounding her?
if you transfix on her radiance long enough
her light seems to spread itself out
overcoming the blackness
that once engulfed her
she seems to shine for herself
not caring who is gazing up at her
if anyone, at all
and so i thought
maybe people
should do the same.

-   s h i n e   f o r   y o u r s e l f

if the universe wants you to notice something
don't be stubborn
it will often grind you down
until you make that change
for your highest good.

- s u r r e n d e r

i saw you
with my fresh eyes
and immediately, undeniably
i felt you in my heart
once again.
i may have forgotten you
for a short while
but my love,
how could i ever really forget
the remarkable way
only you
can make me feel.

- i still feel you here

it's a wonderful feeling
that moment when you realise
what used to cause you
so much hurt
so much emotional pain
to the point you felt drained
of your light, your spark
your fire
no longer has a hold over you
healed at last
entirely free of its grasp
you realise that
your fire
never died
only dwindled, for an instant in time
as a gust of dense darkness
was forced to pass by
but you have triumphed now
deservingly, too
and this is exactly
what you shall continue to do.

    -   y o u a r e f r e e , n o w

isn't it odd?
the comfort we seem to gain
from all the noise
we would much rather sit
throwing meaningless words
to and fro
than experience the dreaded silence
even for just a moment
why do we use our energy
bringing words to life
if their only purpose
is to make a sound?
words should make people feel
leaving our lips to
form bridges
making connections
between souls
instead
we seem to have diminished their value
so when spoken with true passion
too often
they are drowned out
in a sea of white noise.

- be mindful of words

i've died a few times
in my short life
coming back rawer and braver
each time
it was not poetic
it was petrifying
the death of a familiar way of being
tearing all you've ever known
apart
until you are simply left
with yourself
lost in the layers of facades
superimposed over your soul
by society
they are ripped off violently
exposing something you never dared think
to embrace;
that is,
yourself.

- r e b i r t h

quiet
isn't always violent.
isn't always anger.
isn't always moodiness.
stop associating quietness
with negative traits.

yes, sometimes you cross my mind
but that doesn't mean i still
think of you
all the time
after all we endured together
i can hardly be expected to forget
that time
however it's freeing to say,
at last
i can look back at the past
without wanting you back
in my present
for the love i know now in myself
is far more valuable
after all,
you chose not to stay
so i choose now, for myself
to keep it that way.

    -   i t   w a s   n i c e   k n o w i n g   y o u

you really think
you could destroy me?
you underestimate my
magnificence
i have battle scars from wars
fought to reclaim myself
i stood on years of hurt passed
smoothing out the cracks,
grounding my feet
to create a solid foundation
for my life ahead
i am the only person who shall see
my journey
through to the end
and for this reason
nobody
can take me from myself, again.

- r e c l a m a t i o n

a self-love story is the best kind
of love story.

connection is so sacred;
to click with somebody,
to vibe instantly
it's almost like your souls recognise
each other
making for a refreshing encounter
in an often forced
and fragile world.

- t r e a s u r e t h e m

clouds, they wander
through the sky
like stray thoughts passing
through my mind
they shield the sun
they block my view
yet the rays of light
somehow find their way through
the fog has lifted
the end is in sight
but all is different now
for i won't approach it
with fright
fear of what will be
fear of what is not
if we keep beating ourselves up
how can we give life
all we've got?

- finding confidence

strange how those in the same room as us
can seem so distant,
and yet those miles away
can still feel so very close to us
distance can't weaken connection
no, not if it is real
in fact, if it is
it tends to do
the exact opposite.

- d i s t a n c e
  (m a k e s t h e h e a r t g r o w f o n d e r)

those long summer days
with you by my side
stuck in our haze
the world, far from our minds
you wanted to run forever
for a moment, i believed we could
but changes in the weather
meant things didn't unfold
as they should
we loved and we laughed
but you led me astray
now my rose-coloured glasses are off
it seems we lost each other
along the way
we've changed, and
that's fine
so you ran, as i cried
strong arms held me back from you
but your love remains
in my mind.

- j + a

don't you see? love is the point.
if something is not done out of love, then
what value does it truly hold?

be yourself
beautiful and bold
and never apologise for it.

- don't dull yourself down

you try so hard
but you can't change others.
tough though it may be
to come to terms with
only they can do that
and they themselves
must want to.

the problem is
people feel the need to understand
everything
it seems almost impossible for them to
surrender to the fact
not everything needs to be explained
it just is
and maybe
that is exactly
how things are supposed to be.

-   a c c e p t i n g t h e u n k n o w n

usually, those who laugh at the actions of
others, secretly wish they had the courage to
do the same.

my scars
are not signs
of my weakness
but rather evidence
of my resilience.

- scarred, not broken

one thing
i have learned
is that life's true blessings
are usually the completely
unexpected ones
reminding us
that events rarely go
exactly as we plan
and that in itself
can be a strangely beautiful concept.

- let go of control

there was something about the night time that she
adored. maybe it was the fact that nobody expected
anything of her in those hours; under the stars, she
could sit with herself and the moon, finding peace in the
silence that others found eerie.

in my life
i've always wrapped
protective layers around my heart
i don't know
if it's easier that way
but it made sense for me to do so
to keep my warmth inside
in such cold and bitter times
i'm misunderstood
because of it now
and yet
within the right environment
with the right amount of
light and radiance
surrounding me
watch
as i begin to bloom
just like a summer rose
my layers peeling back like fine petals
i'm blossoming into my true and
deepest self
to become beautifully vulnerable
to all those around me.

- w a t c h m e b l o o m

some people never deserved to know you
and that is why they are no longer in
your life.
trust this is for your greatest good.

-   l e a v e t h e m b e

keep going
for the people you have yet to
encounter
that will change your world entirely
keep going
for the experiences you've yet to have
that will cause magic
to surge through your veins
as time seems to stand still
immortalising a single moment
keep going
for the love you will find
and the places you will go
for the people you shall impact
through the highs
and the lows
just keep going
for the best has not been and gone;
as long as you are still breathing
life is sure to keep moving on.

- determination pays off

bravery is leaving someone behind
because you know you should not settle
for anyone
who looks at you for less than what you are;
the universe incarnated,
with two loving eyes
and a strong heartbeat.

- don't settle in fear

she seems at home among nature
not at all out of place
amongst the flowers, trees, birds and bees
sometimes i wonder
if she is truly separate from it,
at all
wandering alone
delicate yet passionate
she seems like a sunflower girl
standing proud and radiating joy
like an infusion of glorious yellow
each and every time
she laughs.

- s u n f l o w e r   g i r l

i think
to have somebody confide in you
bear their heart, their soul
to you
is one of the greatest compliments
one can ever receive.

- be vulnerable with me

we all have that place, i'm sure
where you feel calm
content
where possibilities seem to be endless
you leave a little bit of yourself behind
each time you visit
hoping that way
you will be able to go back,
one day
your home
where you happen not to live
but oh, how you live
whenever you find yourself there
the place where you long to stay
but life
seems to get in the way
yet through memories made
it stays with us,
from day to day.

- the places we leave our hearts

you, reading this
have as much right
as much importance
as much entitlement to respect
as anybody else
stand tall on your own two feet
knowing this
and let nobody
diminish your value
or silence your voice.

- w o r t h

sometimes, it is better to conserve your
energy rather than explain yourself to people.
after all, it is your life and you make your
own decisions; if somebody truly values you,
they will accept them.

sure
be careful who you trust
but just don't forget
that it is okay to
for if you never open up
you may close yourself off
from experiencing deep contentment
through connection with others.

- trusting is beautiful

who are you
when you aren't surrounded
by others?
it's hard
to get you alone
i want to discover the depths of
your soul, and yours alone
i know i will still love you,
afterwards.

- let me unravel your soul

you say you love me
so why can't you show me?
i have learned to trust actions
over words
for i crave a deeper love
than they can scratch the surface of
don't talk to me so much
with your words;
however pretty you can make them
they do not communicate to me
on the level i desire anymore
i want it all or nothing,
yet i feel so lost in between
why can't you take a risk
close your eyes
and let your soul
speak to me?

- before it's too late

i don't always know why
i feel the way i do
but what i do know is
i should never be made
to apologise for it.

-   f r e e t o f e e l

desperation
can make you do things
you promised yourself you
never would.
don't blame yourself,
so very hard.

- mistakes will happen

you are not afraid
you feel afraid
fear does not define you.

- feel it through

and with every tear i cried
over you
the pain gradually left my body
evaporating, saturating
this star-drenched sky
so if you ever look up
do think of me
you can ponder everything
that shall now never be.

- starlight thoughts

anxiety is pointless
and boredom is a killer
so make those plans
bravely follow them through
then thank yourself for
living through love
not fear
for your own deserving happiness.

-   t a k e t h e s t e p

the softer ones who go about
their life
often overlooked, by others
tend to be some of the most interesting people
you shall ever meet.

- universe in our minds

taking advantage of our dreams
feeding off dozens of
pure hearts
i wonder how money can possibly mean
so much to people
as to destroy another's faith in
humanity
as the cost.

-   i s   i t   w o r t h   i t ?

as surely as the night
returns home to the sun
oh my baby
so our time too
shall come.

- p a t i e n c e

when you feel so low
that you can only hope for a miracle
a movie-like scene
to bring you back to life
know that life is not like
the movies
for it tends to have one
subtle difference;
the miracle you need,
it comes from inside
and when the time is right
you shall find your way to it,
and rise.

- your own miracle

once you learn to love your flaws
through the process of knowing yourself
then, you have won.

being manipulated from a young age
can leave you feeling crazy
full of conflicting feelings
blocking out memories,
becoming hazy
but that's just the way it is,
the way it's always been
so go on and take a guess
just why i've become so mean
you find yourself becoming obsessed
just to ensure that your mind doesn't rest
to keep busy and to keep blind
no, i can't stop
i won't fall behind
''you'll figure it out
when you're older''
as i cry,
upon your shoulder
my head feels so full of lies
it's so much easier
to put on this disguise.

she seeks refuge in the power of her
imagination
something she learned from an age too young
to dream of escaping her world so small
to dream that the best was yet to come
blocking out the noise
screwing her eyes up tight
if she lay still long enough
she could make it through the night
learning to keep secrets
she never uttered a word
with a voice so lovely
it's about time she was heard.

- her time is now

indigo and deep
intertwined with stars
it watches those who sleep
overlooking the past
in this moment, too
it shall always be here
holding all the answers
humans struggle to hear.

- mysteries of the universe

the stars do talk
just to those who know
how to listen.

to be down to earth
or to have your head in the
clouds
the secret is simply staying grounded
whilst keeping your eyes on the
sky
at all times.

- l o o k i n g u p

spring is here
bringing with it the chance
for new life
new starts
new perspectives
and as a key part of nature
no doubt this includes you
so there's no time
for fear
as now is your time
to bloom.

-   s p r i n g

so be free, be wild
don't capture yourself;
capture moments,
through living in them.

- here and now

often
people are too wrapped up
in their own lives
to notice what you do with yours
humans can stress so much
about what others
think of them;
we hardly ever look around
to worry about other people's lives
for we are all so consumed by
our own problems
so why not go your own way
make yourself happy
and see how many people
even stop
to question you.

- do what you love

we are not really separate from
this earth;
like flowers
we take in water
which we need to grow
like plants
we need sunlight
to be joyous and to glow
like roots
we must take in nutrients and
support ourselves,
to stay grounded.
as humans we overcomplicate life
so when you need to
take it back to basics
never forgetting that self-care
is vital
for both your vitality and
your happiness.

-   n o u r i s h y o u r s e l f

appreciate what you have
even when you're aiming
for something more
as further advances
come from a sense of abundance
never
from a place of lack.

- you are abundant

sharing an experience with someone
has a curious way of bonding two souls
together.

light as a cloud
you take over my sky
yet your eyes bear tears
like a stormy day
as i wonder what's wrong
you whisper to my surprise
"please, don't go now
and stay, until the sunrise"
you smiled like the sun
and rose from your bed
so the sun shall rise
and life
will go ahead.

-    s u n r i s e

you are magnetic
literally
you attract what you give out your
energy to
so ensure you are cautious
and walk away when
necessary.

-   l a w o f a t t r a c t i o n

our love will stand
the test of time
even if in this life
you cannot be mine
you always find a way
to bring joy into my day
a love like no other
you reach out to me here
through time and space itself
to my heart, above all else
to love from afar,
well it never felt so near
and my soul shall sing silently
each time that you appear.

- s o u l m a t e

if something makes you happy
as long as it's not hurting
anybody
don't let anyone belittle you for it
truth is
they are most likely lacking it
themselves
so be kind, be kind
and if not
leave them be.

- h a p p i n e s s   i s   s a c r e d

everything you want
starts with you
you are always
a good place to start.

- look within

i never know which version
i'm going to get
the man i adore most of all
full of loving wisdom and light
or the suppressed creature
of the night
full of sadness and
dissatisfaction
the more you oppress the latter
the worse, the scarier he emerges
just a drop of that potion
is sure to lure him out
jekyll and hyde
is it really a losing game?
no matter what happens
i know i'll love you,
all the same
but we all know
just how that story ends
can't you see, it's your life
on which this depends.

-   j e k y l l a n d h y d e

change is on the horizon now
we've fought long and hard
to be here,
i know
but now we can relax
embracing all that is to come
for we have made it
and at last
there is nowhere left to run.

- a world to come

the stars are alive tonight
i wonder if you're looking too
i hoped that you might be
to make a wish,
for me and you
all is coming together now
and you seem to have altered time
for though i have not known you long
i feel as though you have always been mine.

- n i g h t s l i k e t h i s

at long last, my darling
you have found your voice
you are blessing everybody
with your intelligence
as well as your presence
and it is oh so beautiful to
witness.

- blossoming

i still miss you
on nights like this
your eyes of blue
and heavenly kiss
it's hard to be strong
when i've been waiting
so long
though make no mistake
for you,
i shall always wait
each heartbreak is worth it
each night spent alone
for all is preparing me
for the day i come home.

- t o y o u

and i still think to feel empty
helpless
is one of the most unpleasant
sensations
something is absent
from your life
you can feel its void within you,
in all that you do
pushing constantly
but you seem to be going nowhere
nobody ever said
it would be easy
and to get what you desire
can seem so far
your heart aches
maybe you needn't try so hard
i know how it hurts, you see
but to take a step back
is not to give up
sometimes,
it is what you need for a while
and if what you want
is what you need
then, with time
it shall find its way to you.

- t r u s t t h e p r o c e s s

they say
you won't achieve anything
by hiding away from life
and avoiding responsibility
but sometimes
this is so necessary
so you can take in the
bigger picture
evaluate
and get ready
to conquer your world.

they sing about love
they write about heartbreak
so beautiful
so bitter
as words try to express
what hearts say.

- w o r d s

i've found that
the less time you spend overthinking
a scenario
the more likely it is
to work out unexpectedly in your
favour.

- k n o w i n g

i dare you
to look in the mirror
acknowledge your beauty
and embrace
all that you are right now
it might sound corny
but you don't want to go
through life
only to look back
one day
to finally realise
how lovely you were
how lovely,
you are.

- s e l f - l o v e

the best revenge
is simply letting go
as this is often
the only way
you will achieve your deserving peace.

- l e a v e i t t o k a r m a

her presence is
light, yet her past
is heavy.

- beautiful contradiction

funny how we care about impressing
those we dislike, as much as we do those
we adore.

so close your eyes
and watch your thoughts
know that they do not define you
as you separate yourself from them
and before you know it
you will have mastered the art of
controlling your mind
letting it dictate your days
no longer.

- free yourself

how powerful it is
to laugh in the face
of your mind's irrational doubt
and do it anyway
just as you always felt
you could.

- c o n q u e r f e a r

why do people say
falling in love
falling pregnant
as if they are
illnesses?
new love and
new life
are these not miracles
that deserve to be
worshipped?

validate yourself, first. you do not
need anybody else to do that for
you.

truth is
you never know what's around the corner
on the next page
but if you did
there'd be no fun in getting up
each day
which is experienced,
always
in a wonderfully unique way.

- s p l e n d i d   u n k n o w n

messed up head
an unfamiliar bed
lying restless above my body
for all i went through
and any hurt
i caused you
i can only say
i'm sorry.

- t r a n s f o r m a t i o n

i began to picture us
in every couple that walked by
and suddenly
it became clear
how you had taken a hold of my mind
but i let it happen
because i loved you so
oh, how i didn't want to be afraid anymore
of a love that otherwise
i may never even know.

- l e t   l o v e   w i n

how can you say
i am not enough for you
and expect me
to apologise?
rather, i pity you
for if you are trying to
use me
to fill the void within you
it is you
who remains incomplete
not i.

don't try to picture
the outcome of it all
instead,
try to picture how you will feel
in that very moment
when all is well
and so, feel it now.

- no fixed outcomes

your eyes
once so bright and glassy
like crystal balls
filled with wonder and intrigue
i could almost catch a glimpse of
our future together
if i focused on them long enough
but now, they seem so hollow
and you barely even meet my gaze
if you value me still
let me know if i'm mistaken
and bring your love
back into my days.

- i just want it to be the same

anything someone pours their entire
soul into is an art in itself,
don't you think?

my dreams
my visions
are so close to my heart
a piece of me entirely
for this is my art
to share with another
is a deep form of intimacy
you see, it can often be
too much
a little too soon
but water me right
and i may just
bloom.

- in good time

listen
there is no right way
and no wrong way
just whatever gets you through
whatever can work
for you.

- y o u r o w n w a y

we throw the word love around
so much
that we seem to have bruised it with
negative connotations
along the way
don't believe them.
to stop loving
is the greatest form of
self-punishment
and you deserve more
much more, than that.

- there is strength in love

sometimes all it takes
is a gesture,
as simple as a smile
and somehow you know
all will work out okay.

- actions speak louder

things are rarely as bad as your
anxiety will lead you to believe.

i dreamt that i met
my younger self, last night
i recall wiping those tears
from her tired, trying eyes
i held her
close to my heart, and said
do not fear, my love
for these times will end
you're a precious flower budding
and one day,
you'll see the light
all that you shall become
could not be, without
this fight.

oh and how
my soul smiled
when instead of waiting
for somebody to save me
finally
i saved myself.

- h e r o i n e

if you fall in love with the little things,
before you know it, you'll have fallen
in love with life.

sometimes i can feel you
in the wind
brushing my face softly
sweeping me off my feet
sometimes i can see you
in my dreams
but i know for now
that is the only place
we can ever meet
sometimes i even hear you
in my laughter
forcing my smile
to grow ever-wider
and as you make yourself known
through all these little things
i don't ache for you
to be by my side
because, my love, you see
you are still here
right now, with me.

- you never left

you came into my life
and showered me with love
i started to think you were a blessing
sent to me,
from above
until you turned like the devil
ripping it all
away
in the name of trust issues
you then refused to stay
but if that wasn't enough
you just had to come back,
for more
to scrape out the depths of my soul
ensuring you got the full taste
before heading for
the door
but you're not worth figuring out
you wonder why,
you have so much pain?
could be karma, i suppose
for you're the very reason that love
has a bad name.

- are you happy, now?

some of the most important things in
life, you cannot see, but by no means
does that mean they are not there.

shooting stars
they pass you by
undeniably fast
yet with a certain splendour
their presence
so easy to miss
gone
if you glance away
just a second too long
but life imitates art
and beauty surrounds us constantly
if only we open our eyes to
notice it
life.
it's happening here and now
so take a look around you,
every once in while
it's the magic passing you by
whilst you're stuck in a trance
of day-to-day life.

- open your eyes

and just sometimes
you realise in a precious moment
it's the seconds like this
we kept going in hope for
manifested into reality
we let them fill our hearts
looking back one day in
nostalgia
turning old feelings into
art.

- the cycle of abundance

it's deeply saddening when
someone is so wrong about you
you don't even know where
to begin
on how to correct them.
especially if they supposedly
care for you.

amidst the uncertainty
of the future
doubt can seep in
through the cracks
of my mind
long buried habits
of living in fear
crawl to the surface
to claim my pride
but then,
a moment of
quiet clarity arises
and my purpose has never felt
as invigorated, or alive;
it's ingrained in my bones
it's a passionate truth
that the product of this
uncertainty
will be sure to see me thrive.

-   s t r e n g t h

and then poetry showed up
pulling all the unsaid words from
my lungs
out onto the paper
until the day came
where i could breathe again.

-   r e l i e f

i want to make my life
as beautiful as possible
decorating it,
with the people i love.

each sunset,
like a grand finale
serenading the day
that shall never be again
as the beautiful bursts of colour
surface to say
their farewells
we are taught to appreciate
the dramatics of nature,
herself.

- s u n s e t

i'm not running away from anything.
i'm just taking back my freedom.

-   l e t   m e   r o a m

oh, no
don't mistake my tears
for weakness.
i know my strength,
i know i'll get through,
just as i always do.
but in order to progress
i must work,
with this sadness;
a détente
from this pointless battle to
be numb
an unlikely alliance forms,
for the betterment of
myself.

- my emotions and i

when your name lit up
my phone,
this evening
no memories came.
no tears of grieving.
instead i laughed,
re-reading your lines
for what a fool you must be
to think i still care
for your kind.

    -   s t a y   g o n e

you cannot force
what is real.

it can be harder to
move on
without the luxury of closure
but thanks to the cowardice
of those who know nothing but
to run
we, for ourselves
must learn to.

- b e t t e r l e f t a l o n e

instead of complaining
about not having enough
be grateful for what
you have;
using it,
to get where you want
to go.

- m i n d s e t

so breathe in the air
letting each breath
renew your essence
filling you
with the strength you need
to try again.

-   c l e a n s i n g

realise the difference
between feeling alone
and being alone;
i feel most lonely
in a room full of people.
i feel most loved
spending time
with myself.

being a girl
attraction is taken as
an invitation
belittlement is expected
and kindness,
abused.
all by those whose
ego-hungry ideals
believe talking down to us
makes them superior.

how the heavens laugh,
at how wrong they are.

- how little they know

it's hard to tell
what's real and what's not
when you feel them both
oh so intensely.

    -   o v e r w h e l m

both innocent
and wild
you cannot be tamed
but possess such rare,
timeless purity
an impossible mix
you tie them together
exquisitely
as the small eyes are
gaping
grasping
failing, to lure you down.

- u n t o u c h a b l e

you share your kindness
like a flower sheds its petals
but don't keep giving up
pieces of yourself
until there's nothing left
for the one who matters most.

-    y o u

the wind kisses my cheek
as the night sky
seems to pull my soul home
into her familiar embrace.

- the comfort of the night

stop thinking so much
and find comfort
in the unexplained.

- r e s t y o u r m i n d

but you see,
i'm so utterly connected to
this earth now
that even my moods
follow the seasons
it's okay,
in the innocent white light
of a summer's day
but as winter falls
the chill in the air
finds its way down my spine
i feel myself freezing over
as if i, too
am withering
to empathise with these plants
around me.

- h u m a n s a n d n a t u r e

break the association
between love and pain
and you will know
freedom.

when life seems to slow down
don't panic about falling behind
instead,
take this moment to realise
where you have arrived
for nothing alive
ever moved at
a constant pace
and by succumbing to
small pleasures,
never a day did
go to waste.

- stop and smell the roses

try not to let confiding in the
wrong people damage your
trust in humanity.

my greatest fear?
one day there'll be
nothing left
to write about.

- at this rate

of course,
when we let people into our hearts
we give them the power
to hurt us,
in exchange
but we never expect them to;
forcing the very thought,
to an untouched corner
of our minds
it's like
a token of trust
they can trade in at
any time
and this is love's risk
which too often
ends with despise.

if someone were to pursue me
out of the blue
i know i'd soon tire
of them
simply as they
aren't you.

- how did you know?

you stole my heart
and i thanked you,
for your crime
for though i am but a
love-struck victim
i'd still give up myself
for you to be mine.

- t o x i c l o v e

i am learning to leave
things that no longer serve me behind
trusting that better doors
will open in response
for after all,
fortune favours the brave
and we must all try to be
just that.

- j o i n m e

sweet november
your love wraps me warm
keeping me alight
my calm,
before the storm.

with this love in my heart
my essence feels renewed
as if the earth is mine to explore
as if there is nothing
i cannot do
with this love in my heart
i am held together,
in strength
for i know what i must do now
and what is waiting for me,
at the end.

-   2 : 2 0 a m

value yourself enough
to pursue what brings you joy in life
anything that gives you a sense of
purpose
of satisfaction
is worth doing;
choose this feeling
above all else.

- and so i wrote the book

the dusk before the dawn made me into the person i am today
the person who wrote this book
ever-changing and ever-growing
tainted, but unbroken

i rise like the dawning of a new day.

Printed in Great Britain
by Amazon

48726768R00121